CAMELS

Susie Dawson

Grolier
an imprint of

www.scholastic.com/librarypublishing

Published 2009 by Grolier
An Imprint of Scholastic Library Publishing
Old Sherman Turnpike
Danbury, Connecticut 06816

© 2009 Grolier

All rights reserved. Except for use in
a review, no part of this book may be
reproduced, stored in a retrieval system,
or transmitted in any form, or by any
means, electronic or mechanical, including
photocopying, recording, or otherwise,
without prior permission of Grolier.

For The Brown Reference Group
Project Editor: Jolyon Goddard
Picture Researchers: Clare Newman, Sophie
Mortimer
Designer: Sarah Williams
Managing Editor: Tim Harris

Volume ISBN-13: 978-0-7172-8060-5
Volume ISBN-10: 0-7172-8060-8

**Library of Congress
Cataloging-in-Publication Data**

Nature's children. Set 6.
    p. cm.
    Includes index.
    ISBN-13: 978-0-7172-8085-8
    ISBN-10: 0-7172-8085-3
    1. Animals--Encyclopedias, Juvenile. 1.
Grolier (Firm)
    QL49.N387 2009
    590.3--dc22
                        2008014675

Printed and bound in China

PICTURE CREDITS

Front Cover: **Shutterstock:** Ramzi Hachicho.

Back Cover: **Shutterstock:** Mario Bruno,
Paul Cowan, Andrejs Jegorovs, Urosr.

Corbis: Sheldan Collins 46, Karen Su 13,
Patrick Ward 16–17, K. M. Westermann 30;
Imagebank: J. Du Boisberran 6, 45, Guido
A. Rossi 21, Robert Seitre 42, Pete Turner 10,
Nevada Wier 38; **NHPA:** Anthony Bannister
22, Douglas Dickins 41, Patrick Fagot 26,
Daniel Heuclin 25, A. F. Papazian 29;
Shutterstock: Vera Bogaerts 34, Mario
Bruno 37, Louise Cukrov 5, Eric Isselée 4,
Karen Kean 9, Hashim Pudiyapura 2–3,
Salamanderman 18, Wilmy van Ulft 33.

Contents

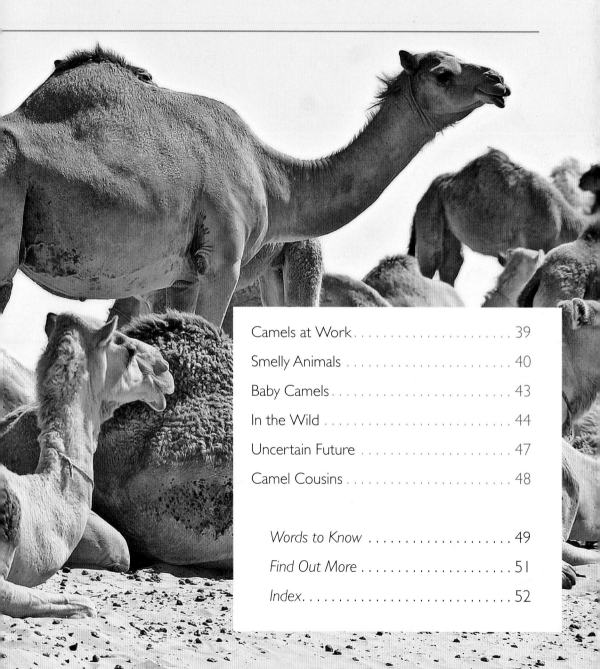

FACT FILE: Camels

Class	Mammals (Mammalia)
Order	Even-toed ungulates (Artiodactyla)
Family	Camel family (Camelidae)
Genus	*Camelus*
Species	Dromedary (*Camelus dromedarius*) and Bactrian camel (*C. bactrianus*)
World distribution	Asia, Africa, and Australia
Habitat	Deserts, dry grasslands, and steppes
Distinctive physical characteristics	Large desert animal; furry coat ranging in color from white to dark brown; one or two humps on back; long curved neck; long thin legs
Habits	Most camels are kept as domestic animals for transport in desert regions; wild camels live in herds, either all male or one male with females and young; camels can go for weeks or even months without drinking
Diet	Desert plants

Introduction

Camels are tough animals. They are one of
the few big animals that can survive in very dry
regions, such as **deserts**. Camels can go without
a drink of water for several weeks.

Camels have a very close relationship with
the people who live in and around the deserts of
Asia and Africa. These strong animals are used
to carry loads and people across the desert. For
that reason, most camels are owned and kept by
humans as domestic animals. There are very few
camels left in the wild.

**Not all camels live in
deserts. These camels
are found in grasslands.**

A camel carries
its owner along
a North African
beach.

Desert Lifeline

Outside their homelands, camels are mainly kept in zoos and wildlife parks. There, people mostly see camels as funny-looking animals with **humps**. However, for millions of people who live in the dry parts of Africa and Asia, the camel is appreciated as an essential part of daily life. The camel supplies these people with almost all the things they need to stay alive—including transportation, milk, wool, leather, and even meat. Without camels, life in the desert for these people would be very difficult, if not impossible.

Camel Basics

A camel is a mammal. It is large, measuring about 7 feet (2 m) high at the top of its hump. You would need to stand on an adult's shoulders just to climb onto its back! At 1,100 pounds (500 kg), it weighs more than five adult men.

A camel has a hump—or two—on its back, a long curved neck, and long legs. Its furry coat varies in color from white to dark brown, but most camels are sandy-beige. Every spring it **molts**—replacing its winter coat with a new, shorter one. On the front of its chest and its knees, it has patches of hard skin on which it rests when it is sitting. Underneath their upper lips, male camels have a single tusklike tooth, which they use for fighting.

Did you know that a camel cannot jump and finds walking in hilly country very difficult?

When a camel runs, it has
a strange swaying rhythm
because the front and
back legs on each side
move together.

Even camels need
a break in the
midday heat of
the Sahara desert.

Desert Home

The camel is unique because it can live in dry desert areas where other large animals cannot find enough food or water. It isn't easy to live in a desert: the sun is baking hot, there is no water to drink, and the few plants that grow are dry and prickly. By midday, the sand is so hot it will burn your skin if you touch it.

The best-known desert of all is the Sahara, which stretches across northern Africa. It is huge—the whole of the United States would fit inside it! Other deserts where camels have lived for thousands of years are the Arabian Desert in the Middle East and the Gobi in central Asia. About 150 years ago, domestic camels were taken to Australia by humans. Some were released into the wild, and others escaped. Now there are herds of **feral** camels living in the deserts of Australia, too.

One Hump or Two?

There are two main kinds of camels. One has one hump and the other has two humps. The one-humped camel is known as an Arabian camel, or **dromedary**. The two-humped camel is called the **Bactrian camel**. Most people just call them camels, without thinking which kind they are talking about.

Nine out of every ten camels alive today are Arabian camels. Therefore, there are many more camels with one hump than there are with two.

The Bactrian camel gets its name from an ancient country where it lived, called Bactria, today part of Afghanistan.

13

Dromedaries

When we think about camels, the dromedary, or Arabian camel, is normally the one that comes to mind. It is slimmer than the Bactrian camel and has longer legs. On its back it has a single hump. Dromedaries can be found in the Middle East, India, and North Africa. They are sometimes called Arabian camels because they lived in a part of the Middle East called Arabia. They are faster than Bactrian camels, although not as sturdy.

Dromedaries are used mostly as **pack animals** but are also good for riding. In the Middle East, camels race against one another, much like horses do in the United States. Camels run at about 10 miles (15 km) per hour. They can keep up a swift, steady speed for more than ten hours.

Bactrian Camels

Bactrian camels are sturdier than dromedaries and have two humps. Their hair is shaggier and darker. The extra hair means they can survive in colder places. They live in deserts and open, windy grasslands called **steppes** all over central Asia. Not all deserts are hot, sandy places. The vast Gobi in Mongolia is very high, and in winter the temperature can drop as low as -40°F (-40°C). The ground is rocky and scattered with large boulders, which is why the feet of the Bactrian camel are hard and leathery.

Almost all Bactrian camels are kept as domestic animals. They are used to carry goods, although there are still a few wild herds. A Bactrian camel wanders along at the leisurely pace of 2 to 3 miles (3 to 5 km) per hour, probably the speed at which you walk home from school. Although slower than a dromedary, it can keep going for longer. Even with a heavy load on its back, it can travel about 30 miles (50 km) a day.

Camel riders line up at the start of a race during the Berber Sahara Festival in Tunisia.

17

This dromedary needs plenty to eat if its hump is to become full again.

18

Inside the Hump

For many years, people thought that a camel carried water in its hump. They thought this was the only way to explain how a camel could survive so long in the desert without drinking. We now know that the hump is in fact a store of fat, not water. All animals store fat in their body, but it is only the camel that has an extra supply in its hump. When the camel has to go without food for long periods in the desert, it uses up the supply of fat in its hump.

A healthy, well-fed camel has a firm hump that weighs about 75 pounds (35 kg). If the camel goes without food for some time, its hump becomes soft and shrinks. However, a few days of eating and drinking are enough to restore the hump to its original size.

Feeling the Heat

We know that the fat stored in a camel's hump will allow the animals to survive for a long time without food in the desert. But what helps a camel cope with the scorching heat?

Camels have very a thick coat of hair on their back. People usually wear a thick coat to keep heat in when it is cold outside. But a thick coat is also surprisingly useful in keeping the heat out. In fact, people who live in deserts wear thick clothes as well.

Camels can let their body temperature rise more than other warm-blooded animals without suffering—by as much as 11°F (6°C). In humans, a rise in body temperature of even one or two degrees is enough to send them to bed and keep them home from school.

Although the desert is very hot in the day, it gets very cold at night. That gives the camel a chance to cool down. Because it is a big animal, it takes a long time to heat up again the next day.

Thick, loose coats help people and camels keep cool in the desert.

The camel's facial features help it survive in the desert.

22

Nose in the Air

What is it exactly that makes a camel look so stuck up? Do you think a camel really is a snob? If a person holds his or her nose in the air like a camel does, they are considered snooty. The features of a camel's face that make it look so superior are just ways it protects itself from the wind and sand of its desert home.

Sandstorms are common in the desert. To keep the sand out of its eyes, the camel keeps its eyelids almost closed and has a double row of long, curly eyelashes. Its nostrils, too, can be closed against the sand, and its mouth kept tightly shut. Now, try doing all this yourself—you will find you have to lift your nose in the air so you can still see ahead of you. It won't take long before you start to look just like a camel.

Chewing the Cud

A camel is a **herbivore**, which means that it eats only plants, not meat. When it has a choice, a camel's favorite foods are grass, wheat, oats, and dates—a sweet fruit that grows in the desert. But if food is hard to find, it will eat almost anything, including dry, prickly plants that other animals won't touch. The prickles don't hurt because a camel's mouth is tough and leathery.

Because most of a camel's food is very tough, it needs a lot of chewing before it can be digested. The first time a camel eats a plant, it starts this chewing then stores the food in a special section of the stomach. Later in the day this partly chewed food is brought back up to the mouth and chewed again. At this stage, it looks a bit like green slime! This time it goes to the other sections of the stomach where it is properly digested. The second kind of chewing is called **"chewing the cud."** Other animals such as cows and deer digest their food in the same way. They are all called **ruminants**.

24

Unlike the goat, the camel must keep its feet on the ground and use its long neck to reach the leaves of desert trees.

If you lead a camel to water, you can be pretty sure that it will drink—a lot!

Thirsty

Camels can go for days or even months without water depending on the time of year. In winter, when there are plenty of juicy plants around, camels get all the water they need from their food and can go for six weeks or longer without a drink. In the heat of the desert summer they need water every three or four days. Whatever the season, they can last ten times longer than humans before they feel thirsty. They can do that not by storing water in their body but by using very little. Most animals keep their body cool by sweating, but this makes them lose valuable water. Camels save water by sweating very little. Also, they are able to lose up to a quarter of their body weight from lack of water without getting sick.

All this does not mean that they don't get thirsty. When a camel arrives at an **oasis** after a long haul across the desert, you would be amazed to see how it drinks! It can swallow about 30 gallons (136 l) in 10 minutes, which is about the same as 500 glasses!

Camels and People

Very few camels live in the wild. Like cows, donkeys, and sheep, camels do not roam free. They have been tamed by humans and kept as domestic animals. Because camels can survive in places with extreme temperatures and few plants, they are very useful to humans. In the harsh environment of the desert, camels and people would not be able to survive without each other.

The camel helps humans in many ways. People help camels by digging wells that provide water for the camel to drink. The only way for people to survive in the desert is to keep constantly on the move, looking for fresh **pasture** for their animals. For this reason, the desert people live in tents, which they can pack up and move once the food in the pasture has run out. People who live this way are called **nomads**.

A desert nomad feeds his camel.

An adult female camel can produce up to 6 pints (2.8 l) of milk each day.

Useful Beasts

The life of the desert nomads is very closely linked to that of the camel. In fact, their language has more than 100 different words to describe the camel. They use every part of the animal to help them survive.

Camel milk is their main food, and camel meat is eaten when a camel dies. Fat melted from the camel's hump is used as butter. Camel wool is woven into cloth, which is used for clothing, blankets, and tents. The skin provides leather for shoes, bags, and saddles. Dried camel bones are carved into jewelry and cooking utensils. Camel dung is dried and burned as fuel. Even camel urine comes in handy. For example, it is used to kill head lice!

Wedding Presents

If you were given a herd of camels as a gift, you might be shocked. But you would feel very differently if you lived in the middle of a vast desert that had no roads or cars for miles in every direction. Camels are so important for desert peoples that they are given as wedding gifts. It's a bit like giving a house or a car in the United States—something that is so important and valuable that it will give you a good start in your married life.

Just as we sometimes guess at a person's wealth based on the kind of car they drive, so the wealth of a desert nomad is shown by the number of camels he owns. Some camels are worth more than others. For example, white camels are very expensive, and camels with strange-shaped humps can always be sold for a higher price.

Camels with white fur are especially sought after by nomads.

33

In addition to people trading camels, goats, and sheep, the Pushkar Fair attracts thousands of tourists.

34

At the Fair

The camel market is the place to visit if you want to buy or sell a camel. Camel markets take place regularly throughout the Middle East and Asia. Because camels are so important, the market is often a local festival.

The largest and most spectacular camel market is the Pushkar Fair, held every November in Pushkar, a town in northern India. People gather from hundreds of villages to meet, trade their camels, and bathe in the holy waters of Pushkar Lake. During the day, beautifully decorated camels are raced and paraded for the crowds. At night, the lake's surface glitters with the light from thousands of tiny oil lamps floating on leaves.

With more than 20,000 camels to choose from, it is usually easy to find someone willing to bargain!

Camel Caravans

Camels have often been called "ships of the desert." Why do you think this might be? Perhaps it's because they carry people and goods across the sand as smoothly and quietly as a ship carries them across the sea. Or maybe because the swaying movement of a camel is said to make its passenger feel "seasick."

People have used camels for transportation across deserts for thousands of years. The camels can travel long distances with little food or water. Their feet have soft pads on the bottom that act a bit like snowshoes and prevent them from sinking into the sand when they walk. Dromedaries can carry a load of 220 pounds (100 kg) for a distance of about 20 miles (30 km) a day.

A long line of loaded camels traveling across a desert is known as a **caravan**. It was from this earliest kind of mobile home that we got our modern meaning of the word caravan.

A camel caravan makes its way into camp.

In China, Bactrian camels are used to carry crops back from the fields at harvest time.

Camels at Work

In general, it is the male, or bull, camels that are used to carry heavy loads. The female camels, called cows, are better for riding. Camels are usually quite **docile**, but like most of us, they don't always work without complaining. They may howl loudly when the load is put on their back. If the load is too heavy, they will sit down and refuse to move.

Camels cannot wear a bit and bridle like a horse because their mouth must be free to chew the cud. Instead, a rope is put through a hole near the camel's nose. The camel is given commands by being spoken to and guided with a stick. At night, the camels have their front legs tied loosely together so that they can only take very short strides. In this way, they are free to **graze** around the camp without being able to escape.

Smelly Animals

Have you read the wonderful story "How the Camel Got His Hump" by Rudyard Kipling? In the story, the camel got his hump as a punishment for being very lazy. The hump meant that he could then work twice as hard as the other animals because he no longer needed to stop for food.

There seem to be great differences of opinion about the temperament of camels. Some people see them as noble and hard-working, while others think of them as stubborn, lazy, and stupid.

The only thing about which there is no argument is that camels are very smelly! They are also quite unpredictable. All camels may kick and bite when upset, and Bactrian camels even spit at people. If you want to know when a camel is upset, look at its ears—if they are pressed back close to its head, stay clear!

**Stand back!
This camel is
very upset.**

41

The new baby is very unsteady at first, but within a few hours it will be able to keep up with its mother.

Baby Camels

Like humans, camels usually have only one baby at a time. The female, or cow, camel gives birth after a 13-month pregnancy. She quickly helps the baby, or calf, to its feet and gives it its first drink. Although the baby camel takes milk from its mother for about a year, it also starts to nibble plants right from the beginning. The mother and calf like to stay close together. They call to each other if they get separated.

The carefree life of a baby camel ends when it is one year old. From then on, it has to start its training. First it learns how to stand and kneel on command. It is also given small packs to carry. By the age of five years it is fully grown and must carry a full load.

Female camels have babies every two years. Since camels live to be about 30 years old, a female camel will probably have about 12 calves in her lifetime.

In the Wild

Humans have been taming camels for at least
4,000 years, so there are very few camels living
in the wild today. A few herds of Bactrian camels
run wild in the Gobi, and herds of dromedaries
roam in Australia.

In their natural state, camels live in herds of
up to 30 animals. There are two kinds of herds.
They are either made up entirely of adult males,
or they have one male, 10 to 15 females, and
their young.

Because camels are herd animals, it is
difficult to persuade a single camel to start
out on a journey on its own. They definitely
prefer to travel in groups.

A group of wild
dromedaries starts
out across the
Australian desert.

**Trucks and dromedaries
share a road in the
Sahara desert.**

Uncertain Future

It is thought that there are about 12 million dromedaries in the world. Their numbers are decreasing in some countries, but all over the world the camel population has stayed about the same. This means that there is no immediate threat to their survival. Bactrian camels are much rarer. They only live in harsh areas such as the Gobi, where they are vulnerable to droughts and freezing winters.

The future of camels is very closely linked to the future of desert nomads. Earning a living in the desert is hard, so more and more nomads are choosing to settle in cities and give up the nomadic way of life. For those who remain in the desert, many roads have been built. If you could afford a truck, which would you prefer, a truck or a camel to carry you across the desert? Which do you think would be faster? Which would be more reliable? The desert people themselves choose to have both. It seems that trucks and camels are both useful but in different ways.

Camel Cousins

Animals that are similar but not exactly the same are grouped together in animal families. There are six different members, or species, of the camel family. Two of them have already been described in this book—the dromedary and the Bactrian camel. The other members of the family all live in the mountains of South America. Try to imagine a very small camel with no hump. That is what the camel's closest relations look like.

The best-known camel relative is the **llama**. Like the camel, it is used mainly as a pack animal. The other three relatives of the camel are much like the llama. They are the vicuña, the guanaco, and the alpaca. The alpaca has long woolly hair, and its name is also used to describe the wool made from this hair.

Because of their usefulness, llamas and alpacas—like domestic camels—will probably always be used by people. Guanacos and vicuñas, however, need protection from loss of their natural habitat and illegal hunting.

Words to Know

Bactrian camel   A camel with two humps that lives in central Asia.

Caravan   A group of people and animals who travel in a long line.

Chewing the cud   Chewing food that has been brought back to the mouth having already been swallowed once.

Deserts   Sandy areas with few plants. They become like that because there is very little rain.

Docile   Quiet and obedient.

Dromedary   A camel with one hump that lives in the Middle East and North Africa. It is also called an Arabian camel.

Feral   Wild once again after being domesticated by humans.

Graze   To eat grass or plants.

Herbivore   An animal that eats only plants, not meat.

Humps Large lumps on the back of camels in which fat is stored.

Llama A member of the camel family that lives in South America. It is smaller than a camel and has no hump.

Molts Sheds a coat of fur and then grows a new coat.

Nomads People who constantly move from place to place.

Oasis A place in the desert where there is water.

Pack animals Animals used for carrying things, usually over rough ground where no wheeled vehicles can go.

Pasture Land that has grass or plants for animals to eat.

Ruminants Animals that chew their food more than once.

Steppes Flat, grassy areas with no trees. Steppes are mostly found in central Asia.

Find Out More

Books

Stevens, K. *Camels*. New Naturebooks. Mankato, Minnesota: Child's World, Inc., 2007.

Wexo, J, B. *Camels*. Zoobooks Series. Poway, California: Wildlife Education, Ltd., 2001.

Web sites

Arabian Camel or Dromedary
www.enchantedlearning.com/subjects/mammals/camel/
Camelcoloring.shtml
Facts about the Arabian camel and a picture to print.

Bactrian Camel
www.enchantedlearning.com/subjects/mammals/camel/
Bactrian.shtml
Information on Bactrian camels and a picture to print.

Index

 W9-BXT-407